A Survival Guide for Landlocked Mermaids

A Survival Guide for Landlocked Mermaids

Margot Datz

ATRIA BOOKS
New York London Toronto Sydney

BEYOND WORDS
PUBLISHING

For my art teachers,
Marion Hammel and *William Haust*, who taught me that
these mysterious things on my back were actually wings.

ATRIA BOOKS

A Division of Simon & Schuster, Inc.
1230 Avenue of the Americas
New York, NY 10020

20827 N.W. Cornell Road, Suite 500
Hillsboro, Oregon 97124-9808
503-531-8700 / 503-531-8773 fax
www.beyondword.com

Copy editor: Julie Steigerwaldt
Managing editor: Lindsay S. Brown
Cover: Carol Sibley and Sara E. Blum
Interior design: Sara E. Blum
Technical assistants: Pictex Studio
Photography assistants: Ron Hall

First Atria Books/Beyond Words hardcover edition April 2008

ATRIA BOOKS and colophon are trademarks of Simon & Schuster, Inc.
Beyond Words Publishing is a division of Simon & Schuster, Inc.

For more information about special discounts for bulk purchases, please contact
Simon & Schuster Special Sales at 1-800-456-6798 or business@simonandschuster.com.

Manufactured in China

10 9 8 7 6 5 4 3 2 1

Library of Congress Cataloging-in-Publication Data:

Datz, Margot.
  A survival guide for landlocked mermaids / Margot Datz. -- Atria Books/Beyond Words 1st
hardcover ed.
    p.   cm.
1. Datz, Margot. 2. Women--Psychology. I. Title.

  NC975.5.D38A4 2008
  155.3'33--dc22

                            2007019859

ISBN-13: 978-1-58270-160-8
ISBN-10:   1-58270-160-1

The corporate mission of Beyond Words Publishing, Inc.: *Inspire to Integrity*

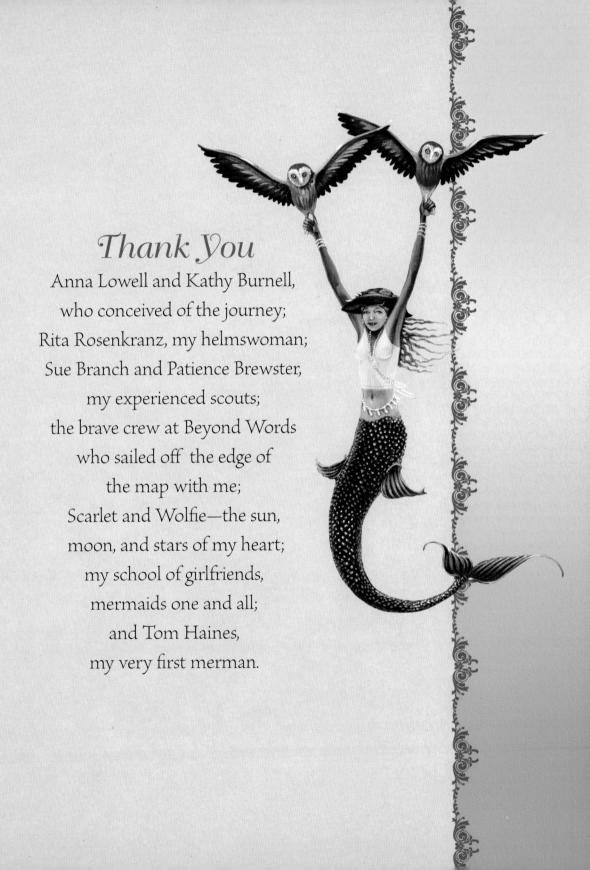

Thank You

Anna Lowell and Kathy Burnell,
who conceived of the journey;
Rita Rosenkranz, my helmswoman;
Sue Branch and Patience Brewster,
my experienced scouts;
the brave crew at Beyond Words
who sailed off the edge of
the map with me;
Scarlet and Wolfie—the sun,
moon, and stars of my heart;
my school of girlfriends,
mermaids one and all;
and Tom Haines,
my very first merman.

Cherries

Introduction

Darwin may have been quite correct in his theory that man descended from the apes of the forest, but surely woman rose up from the frothy sea, as resplendent as Aphrodite on her scalloped chariot. These early mermaids, once content below the waves, came up for air to scan the horizon and then plunged back down to sustenance and safety.

What drove us from our watery sanctuary onto dry land? Like other sea life, mermaids were evolving too. And mermen had become quite rare, private, and in great demand. When mermaids tried to expand their mating options, enticing men into their aquatic territory, the poor fellows had a tendency to sink, rendering them, sadly, rather dead. So we mermaids abandoned our natural psychic habitat to seek mates on shore, and we have been like fish out of water ever since.

We've adapted admirably to our landlocked circumstances, mastering most of the skills of landfolk, and managing, with much effort, to "fit in." But the mermaid within longs to slip on her tail from time to time and vanish beneath the curl of a breaker, leaving behind her unwashed dishes. We yearn to be fully immersed in the weightless world of our free spirit's true home, where our playful natures return to us with each sweep of our fantails, and protocol is silenced by a far more joyful call of the sea. We want to be refreshed, to remember, to find our way back to the part of us that is mostly ocean.

Some women have forgotten their primal origins and have donned the way of man, adjusting to civilization's formalities and institutions. Others recall their nature but feel alone and odd, veiling their restlessness and suppressing their impulses. Sighs wash over them like the lapping shores. There are, however, an increasing number of mermaids that are growing their tails back, and they know how to use them!

*P*erhaps you feel the stirrings of a wild feminine creature within, a longing to leap out of the fishbowl of familiarity into the turbulent unknown. Do you wonder if other women feel as mischievous and unruly as you often do? Do they delight in the same fantasies you've stashed away for another more "appropriate" time? Maybe you faintly remember what it is to *really* play . . . Do you recall the reckless fun of tumbling head over tail fin in the lathering rips of cross tides with water diamonds sparkling all around you? It is time to remember Mother Ocean's arms that rocked you, and who you really are.

*T*his is a handbook for the landlocked mermaid, survival tips for the stranded sea nymph's soul. She is the essence of playful femininity, coaxed from the safety of the Great Mother Ocean. Inside us she swims around in circles, longing for bigger waters. Her care and feeding unfurl in these pages. Run a bath, put your tail up, let your hair down, and slip into a comfortable mood. Your dormant mermaid is about to receive the kiss of life.

Dare to Be Bare

The only way to be a mermaid is to be true to yourself, which means you've got to dare to be bare. That is, to bare your heart and soul. Head up, chest out, tail fanned. It's not easy being yourself because it can invite envy and attention. But if you hide your authentic self from the rest of the world, a unique life will pass you by. There is a splendor in being true to yourself. Another perk: you draw your own kind to you. Suddenly, you're not the only mermaid in the sea.

She Tried Very Hard to Fit In

She Was Trying to Remember the Last Time She'd Had a Really Good Swim

Never Lose Sight of the Sea

Mermaids must never lose sight of the sea—their instinctive home. Losing sight of our instincts landlocks us into routine and drudgery. It's like trying to waltz with an anchor. When we plunge into our instincts, our unconscious speaks to us in dreams, hunches, and unexplainable impulses. Like the language of dolphins, it is foreign to the untrained ear, but in the underwater world, it carries great intelligence.

Seek the Company of Other Mermaids

If there's one thing mermaids know, it's that they have more fun. Mermaids never betray each other. They know it's a sisterhood, not a competition. Mermaids encourage and compliment each other, swooning over their achievements and beauty. They give each other gifts that glorify their kindred spirits. The more mermaids, the merrier. In our natural state, we form great whirling schools of harmony and beauty.

The Great Gathering

Moonlight Foxtrot

Allure for Sure!

Mermaids come in all shapes and sizes. And they can be knock-down, drag-out sexy whenever they feel like it. Mermaids give each other permission to frolic, glob on the pearls, pump up the push-up bras, douse themselves with perfume, and dance. Their sexiness is a celebration of themselves from head to tail, and they do it all for themselves. A mermaid can make a barnacle blush. She cannot be shamed for her inner or outer beauty and so shares it with the world. Truly loving herself is the secret to her allure.

Fire and Water Don't Mix

A few great advances resulted from the mermaids' land migration. Some of them learned the richly rewarding art of cooking. Attempts at cooking underwater failed miserably and never really amounted to much more than sushi. But it's another matter on terra firma. Mermaids like to eat, drink, and be ridiculous! And all of them have to agree that lobster tastes waaaaay better cooked. Mermaids love to entertain other mermaids and have been spotted line dancing en masse in the moonlight.

When It Came Down to Birthdays, There Was No Stopping Great-Aunt Tallulah

She Wore Many Hats

Accessorize, Accessorize, Accessorize

At times it's the small things
that give way to the big things. The
pleasure of expressing your essence
through dress excites others to join you
in the flamboyant, playful act of being
original. By revealing who you are and
how you feel, you send out waves of
beauty and excitement wherever you
are. Mermaids may not wear blouses at
all times, but be assured they wear many
hats for many moods. Mermaids aren't
timid about color or styles. These are just
more ways to let the fun begin!

Even Mermaids Get the Blues

A tiny bit of ocean leaves our bodies when we cry. It reminds us of our origin: the clear blue sea of awareness. An awareness so painful at times, that our eyes long to shut, and our ears yearn for silence. Sadness can run a mermaid aground on the mudflats of despair. But her tears make the ocean deeper.

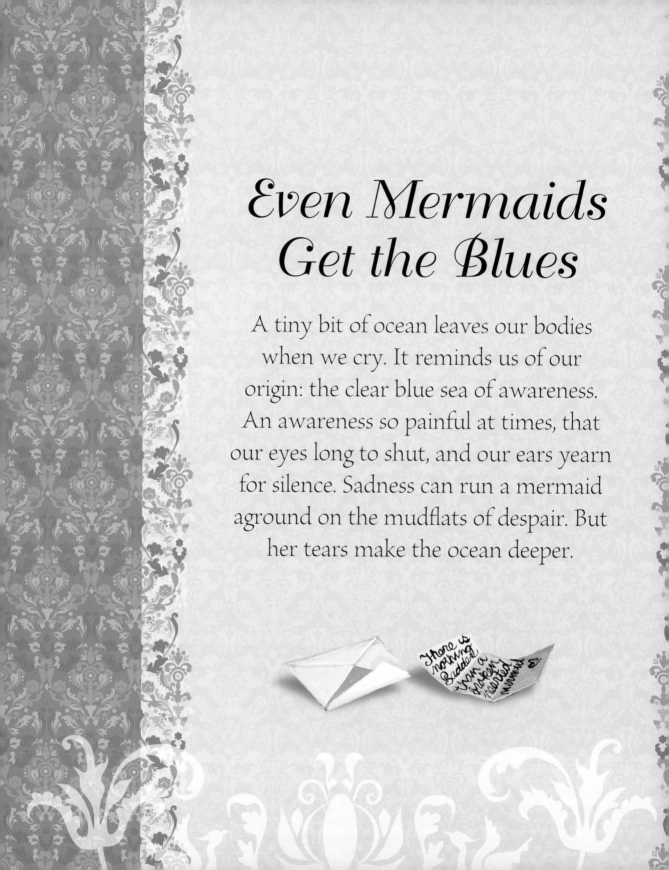

There is nothing sadder than a broken hearted mermaid

There's Nothing Sadder Than a Brokenhearted Mermaid

Reflection

Cultured Pearls

Being true to your inner mermaid often collides with culture. Culture has a lot of helpful guidelines (i.e. codes, creeds, and commandments) that direct her toward "appropriate behavior." Unfortunately, all a mermaid has to do to conform is cut off her tail. She does this when she pretends to be other than what she is. The worst form of pretending is when she pretends even to herself. The shoreline between culture and the truth may vacillate, but a mermaid knows the difference.

Learn to Yearn

A landlocked mermaid is filled with longings. She yearns for the part of her she had to leave behind and for all that she might become. She yearns for beauty, freedom, and love. Yearnings are the navigational stars of the visionary and precede the sojourn to fulfillment.

She Could Not Explain Her Obsession for Shoes

Miss Priss and Ms. B. Havior Have a Little Chat

The Dark of the Moon

Deeply influenced by the tides, mermaids revere the moon. They love the night's waters, highlighted with platinum and dappled with diamonds. They understand the true need for darkness in nature … and themselves. Their most sensual aspects arise out of their nocturnal pools. Have you ever seen a mermaid's lingerie? She invented fishnet stockings! She put the naughty in nautical!

The Importance of Pearls

Mermaids can never have enough pearls. Swags and festoons of them drape and drip from their hair, neck, and arms. Each pearl is a jewel of wisdom, wrestled from struggle and strung in sequence to create infinite insight and compassion for the mermaid who wears them. The older the mermaid, the more pearls. Darling, it's only fair! Young mermaids begin their search for pearls and never cease until they've culled every oyster.

She Sought the Advice of an Older Mermaid

She Had to Admit, She Had a Fish's Tail and Crow's-Feet

Crow's-Feet and Fish Tails

Mermaids never die, but they do age. Aging is cause for reflection. Gaze into the mirror of self-examination, but don't get stuck there criticizing every imperfection. Mermaids respect aging and recognize it as their destiny. They already have a fish tail—why not crow's-feet? A mermaid's eternal spirit keeps her buoyant.

Cultivate an Inner Water Garden

Gardens are no accident. They are created with affection, care, and patience. Each of us needs a pure, quiet sanctuary within, an inner spiritual realm to which we can retreat. We cultivate this garden with prayer and meditation. The weeding of negativity and the propagation of flowering thoughts requires daily visits. Each prayer plants a lotus in your lily pond of peace.

Balinese Mermaid

Shedding

No Dreading Shedding

Mermaids are psychologically complex. They are part conscious, part unconscious. Sometimes the underwater part of them sheds old habits and perceptions, making way for transformation. It's a deep blue process that starts from within—one that can't always be explained, even to those we love. But a mermaid trusts life and its mysteries and survives sea changes.

Work with the Tides

At times, the moon's jurisdiction can
be far mightier than our own wills,
and mermaids may tatter their tails
swimming against the tides. When forces
are unfavorable, time wears on, and the
ebb of circumstances can be draining.
A wise mermaid knows her waves will
come as she rides the riptides and rolls
with the undertow. When the tides of
good fortune gush back, her struggles
are soon forgotten. She knows her
waves will come.

Riding the Waves

When the Moon Was Full She Felt the Tug of the Tide

Improvise Oceans

When tidal waves of stress wash you ashore and you're crawling along like a gasping lungfish, it's time to create a makeshift sea. Run a bath and sink down deep. Dunk your head underwater and revitalize your halo. Stay in long enough to get your shimmer back. And drink water—it keeps a mermaid juicy. A stressed-out siren resembles salt cod more than a sea goddess.

Heads versus Tails

A respectable landlocked mermaid appears to lead with her head. However, were you to overhear her thoughts, you would note an ongoing argument maintained with her tail, which has a small mind of its own! A mermaid is not frightened by her own duality. She is a walking contradiction of piety and lust, sobriety and ecstasy, brilliance and stubbornness, the sacred and the scandalous. The tug between the tail and the head is at the very core of our own evolution toward inner harmony. Duality dwells at the heart of all truth, so dance with your own inner paradox.

Something About Him Made Her Want to Be Naughty

The Keeper

Ahoy There, Mate!

Once your inner mermaid is as frisky as Flipper, the idea of flipping for someone may not be a bad one. In fact, it's one reason why mermaids came ashore in the first place. Just as there are many fish in the sea, there are many men on land, and a mermaid must be discerning. She bravely enters courtship with her senses alert. There's nothing like love. It's worth all the storm surges and slack tides that go with it. Permission to come aboard!

Let Your Love Light Shine

Mermaids need to be wily for many good reasons. Their allure attracts all types—heartbreakers and sweethearts alike. Mermaids must be discriminating, but when true attraction strikes, it doesn't hurt to let the lucky fellow know. Shine your light on him, splash your tail, and rock his boat!

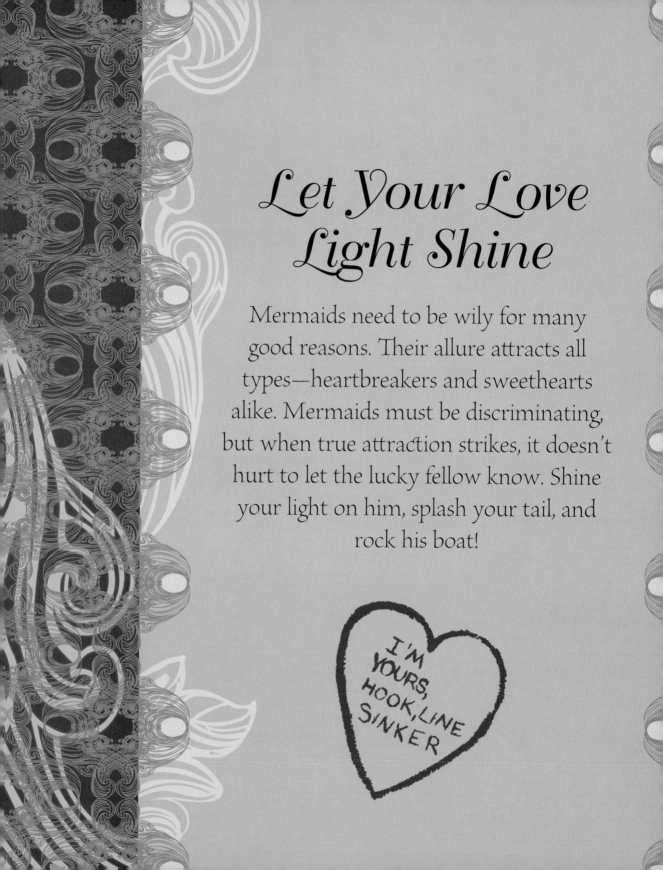

I'M YOURS, HOOK, LINE SINKER

Apprehending the Vandal

Moonlighting

Learn Seamanship

Men of the sea heed the call of the wild, and their passion generates a magnetism that mermaids find irresistible. Sailors, whalers, fishermen, and pirates work the waters in their own fashion. Sailors skim the surface, their main sails filled with gusts of great intention. Their gaze is on the North Star, and their goal is just over the horizon. And there you are, a landlocked mermaid, left ashore to tend the hearth. Hmmm. Perhaps it's time to take sailing lessons while he learns to swim.

Fishermen

It's hard for any fisherman to resist angling for a mermaid. They'll do everything they can to land us. Then they bring us home to show us off to their friends. But a lot of these seamen don't know about the care and feeding of mermaids. To be captured as a trophy and then have our emotions neglected is tragic. We might as well be stuffed and mounted on a wall! A smart mermaid knows her needs. However tempting the bait, she can spot a long line ten leagues away. Her sonar is savvy. She has no intention of being kept in a lonely fishbowl.

Waiting for Her Ship to Come In

Many brave men are asleep in the deep.

So beware, Beeeware

Davy Jones's Locker

Pirates

Pirates are the bad boys of the boating world. They party hardy and rabble-rouse with the best of them. However, they are thieves at heart, and your heart may be their next heist. To be pillaged and plundered emotionally maroons a loving mermaid on an island of despair. So beware, beware. Just what don't you understand about the skull and crossbones?

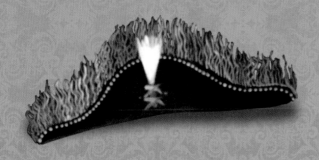

Beware of Strangers Bearing Crustaceans

All the lobster in the world cannot lure a mermaid out of her shell if she suspects insincerity. Courtship can be intoxicating, clouding a mermaid's judgment. A wise mermaid always looks a gift sea horse in the mouth. Remember, many characters lack character. Watch for the difference.

She Was the Kind of Woman You Courted with Crustaceans

Merlovers

Mermen

The rarest men are the mermen. These triumphs of nature lived full lives above water and partook of all the manly ways. Yet something lacked in their lives, a depth of soul and emotional experience, which left them in the brackish stagnant pools of existence. It was there that they heard the laughter of the mermaids, the sirens' song of invitation to join them in the waves. Many men have drowned in the arms of lonely mermaids who did not comprehend their mates' need to breathe. Their impatience led to their men's demise. But a few marvelous men merged with the sea and became great psychic swimmers. These are the mermaids' true soul mates, and their love plumbs the depths of emotion. Together they are free.

Hook, Line, and Sinker

Commitment is the knot that binds us. No matter how many niceties you may share, your differences will create tension. Adversity can strengthen the knot, if the lines of communication are tied securely. A solid commitment splices two lives together and holds through the storms.

Everyone Thought They Had So Much in Common

The Wreck of the Good Ship Matrimony

Sea Witches

Not all mermaids are good. Some mermaids went awry. They stayed on land a little too long, and their hearts dried up, their tails dropped off, and their souls shriveled. These are the sea hags that cry to ships and tempt men onto the jagged reefs, devouring them as they drown. They give mermaids a very bad name.

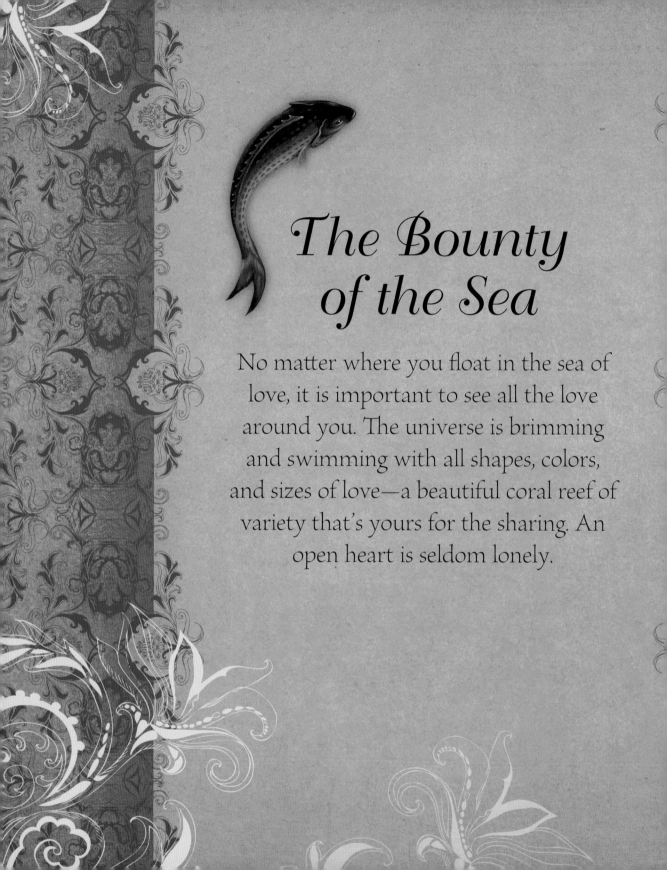

The Bounty of the Sea

No matter where you float in the sea of love, it is important to see all the love around you. The universe is brimming and swimming with all shapes, colors, and sizes of love—a beautiful coral reef of variety that's yours for the sharing. An open heart is seldom lonely.

Despite Her Attempts at Conversation, He Had One Thing on His Mind

Mermother

Mermothers

Some mermaids choose to become mermoms. It's not for every mermaid, but a grand and joyful choice for many. Mothering is demanding, to say the least, but mermothers have an extra splash of intuition to help them along the way. Child rearing requires many strengths: common sense, patience, compassion, wisdom, and humor, to name a few. If mermothers ever find these in short supply, they get support from their own mothers and other fellow mermothers. And they become finer mothers for it.

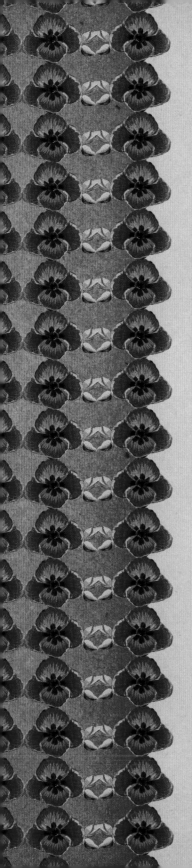

Never Let Go of Your Mermaid's Pocketbook

Scattered along the shore, in tangles of seaweed and crab shells, are the black, twining skate egg cases known as "mermaid's pocketbooks." They appear as though their straps had broken and their contents had strewn. They lay abandoned, cast off by some aquatic purse snatcher. Hold on tight to your mermaid's pocketbook. There are those who would wish to pick at your credibility, steal your values, or forge your identity. Hang on to your integrity and misbehave with dignity.

Marlaina Walks Her Dog

Stream of Consciousness

Mermaid's Lullaby

Big Mama Ocean teaches us the rhythms of life. Each tide ebbs and flows, leaving its jetsam and flotsam. Each wave crests and troughs. Our bodies are infused with these cycles. We inhale and exhale, wake and sleep. Even our souls sway in the give and take of all things, as the ocean quietly chants to our hearts:

Love one another
Love yourself
Love one another
Love yourself
Love one another
Love yourself

To
Thine
Own
Mermaid
Be
True

Dawn

Photo: Ronald Hall

Margot Datz began her career in sculpture, which soon developed into a love of murals, trompe l'oeil, decorative painting, and interior design. The self-taught painter embellishes the walls of hundreds of homes and businesses, on and off Martha's Vineyard, as well as her eighty-five-foot mural and bas-relief installation for the Arkansas Children's Hospital. In addition to her murals, framed paintings, and print series, she has illustrated four children's books for longtime friend Carly Simon.

Margot's painting style blends her own whimsical, indigenous iconography with lighthouses, sailors, fishermen, mermaids, and the ever-present blue sea. She has been featured in national publications such as *Architectural Digest, House & Garden, Home, In Style, Romantic Homes,* and *The New York Times,* and has appeared on CNN and NPR's *All Things Considered.* She lives with her pet dog Yoda, a hairless Chinese Crested, on Martha's Vineyard.

To learn more about Margot and her work, visit her website at www.margotdatz.com.